I0475170

Easy To Hard, Mandala Art Therapy Adult Coloring Book
For seniors, children and beginners of all ages

Copy Rights

Table Of Contents

Introduction

Coloring books have been around since the late 1800's. Today's art books have made a turn most people did not expect. These fascinating colouring sheets actually started clubs of dedicated fans and collectors all around the world in a matter of a few short years.

This in itself shows us that they do have an affect on our lives by helping us to reduce stress levels, calm a busy mind, become more creative and simply allow us to relax in this hectic world we live in each day.

Our adult colouring book contains original geometric shapes using the natural earth triggering Mandala art. The math that creates a perfect spiral in a shell or the spectacular lines of a diamond are gifts from mother earth to us.

Test Page For Chosen Medium

Please test the medium that you have chosen to color with on the following blank page. Be it ink pens, felt tips, watercolours or other. I have provided an additional three blank pages at the end of this book for extra test paper. We have also used a blank page between art so you may carefully remove the page into a frame if need be for a gift idea or easy art for the walls of your home.

Test Page Here

Use the space below to test colors and your mediums weight before you start.

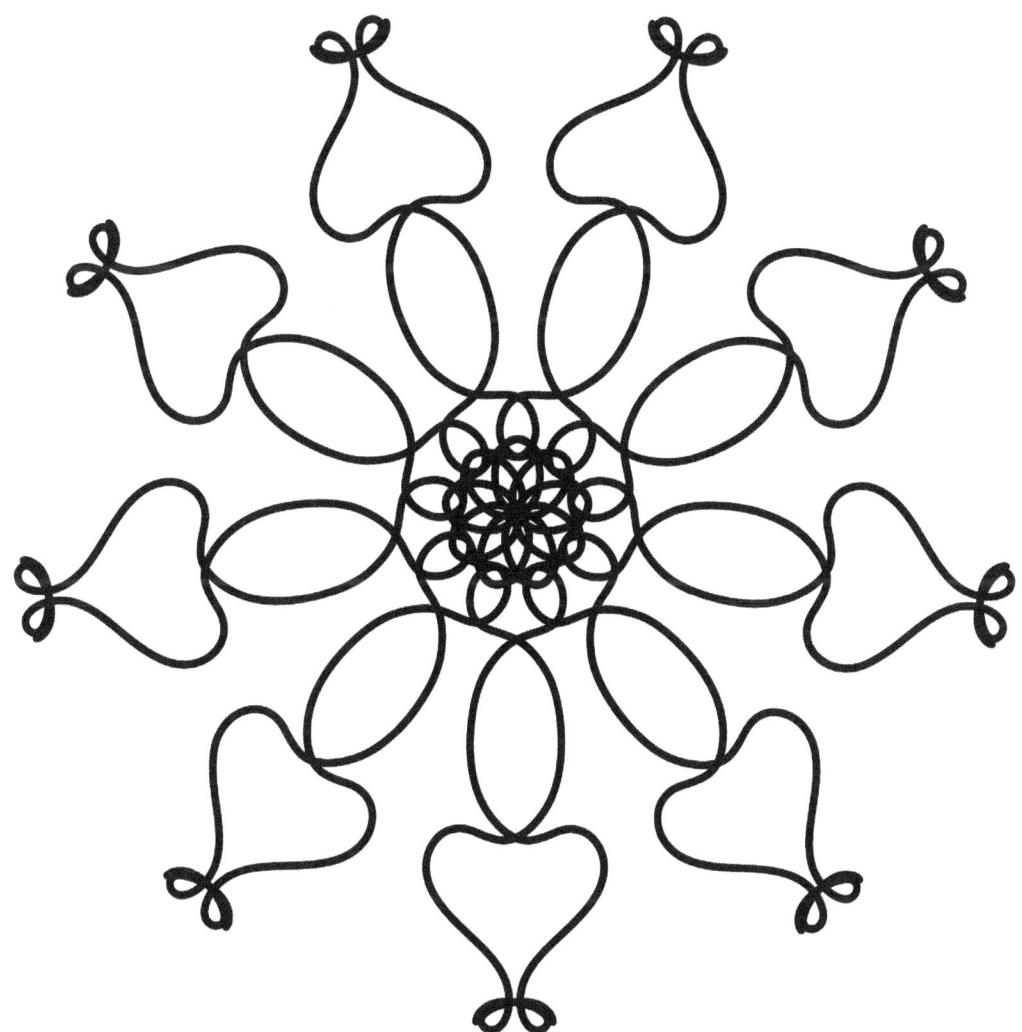

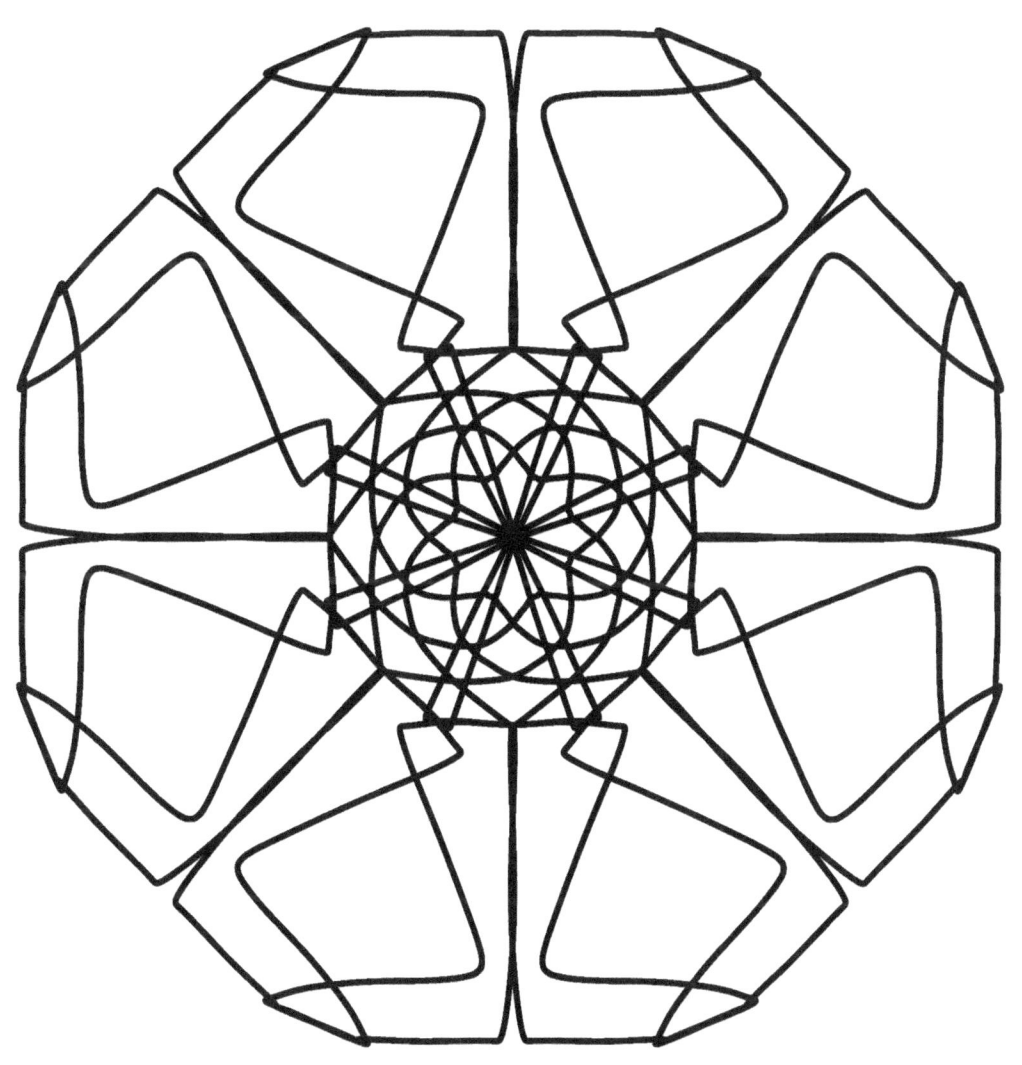

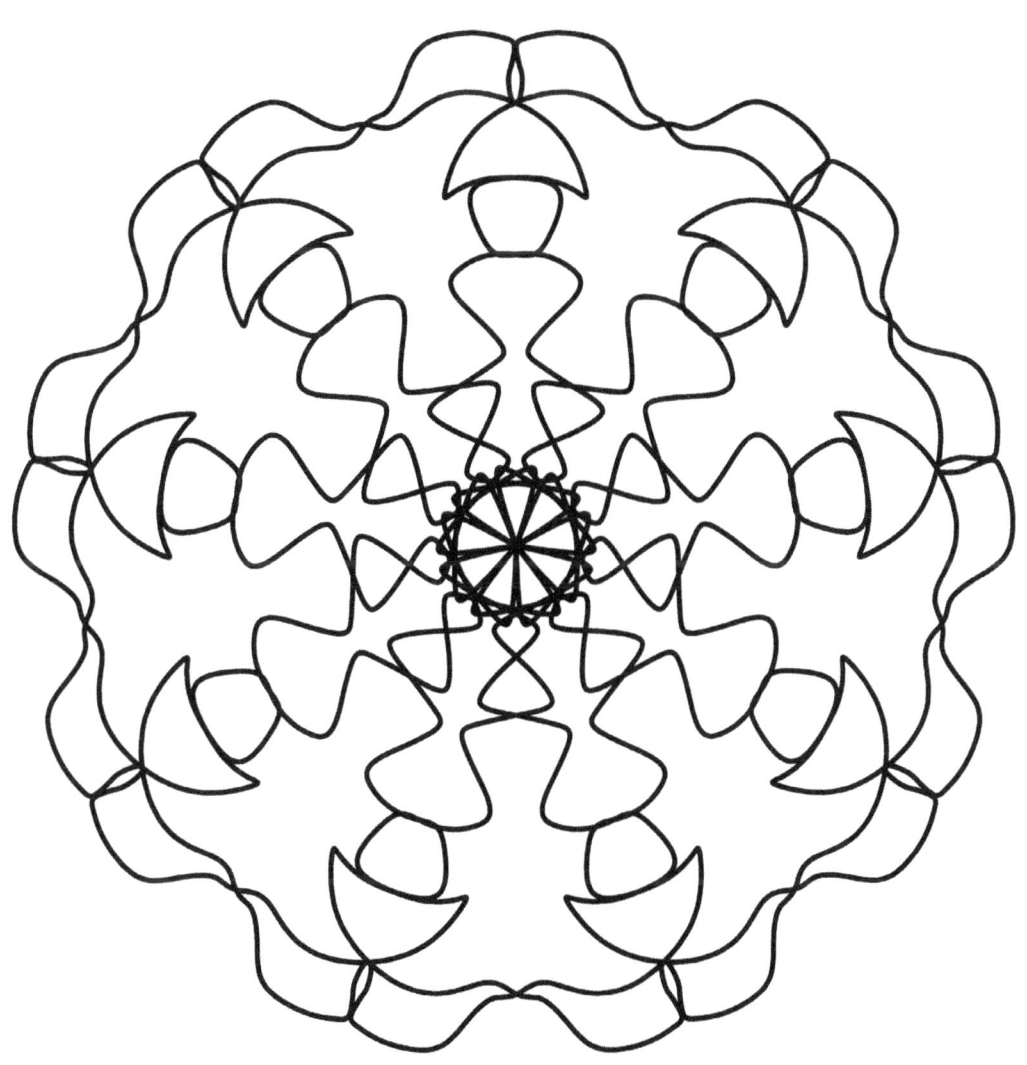

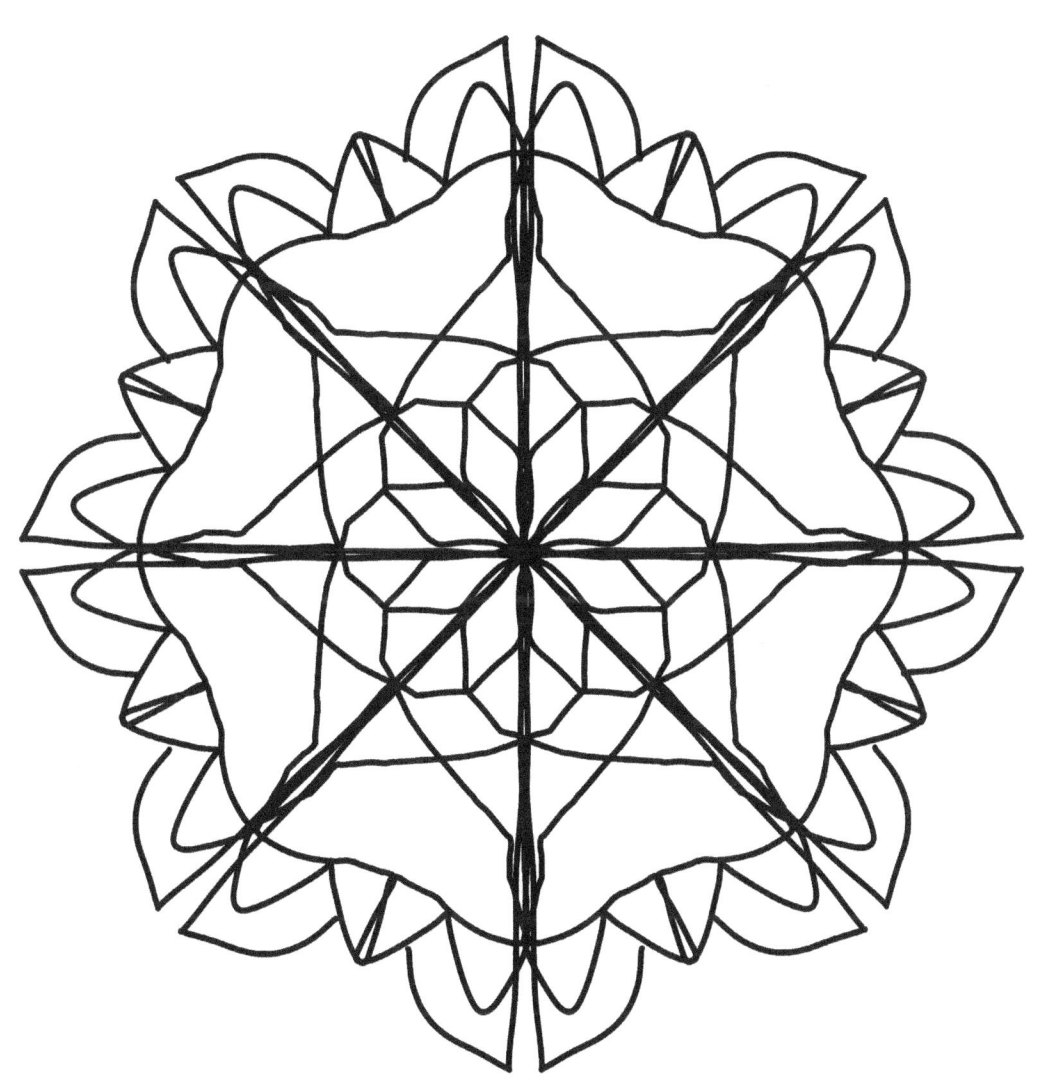

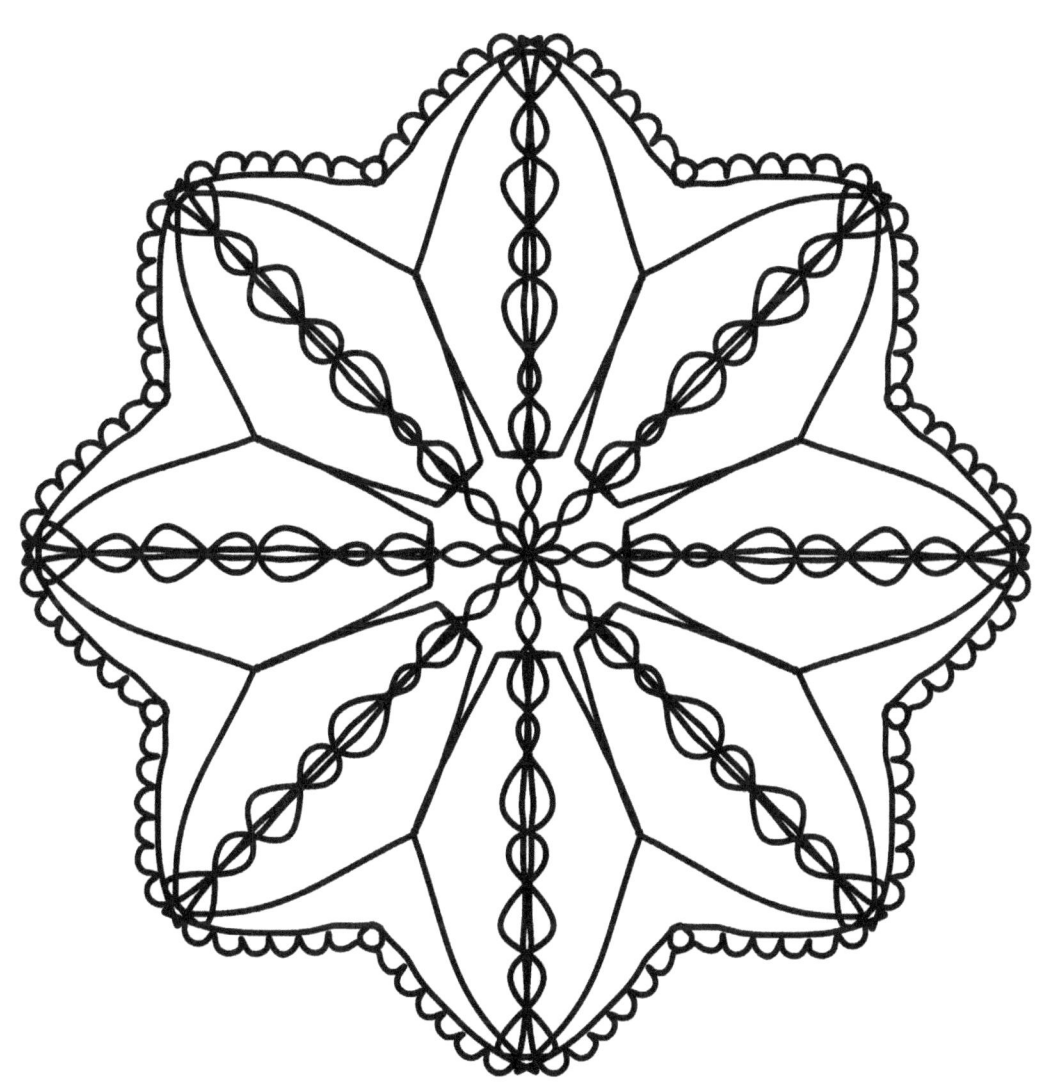

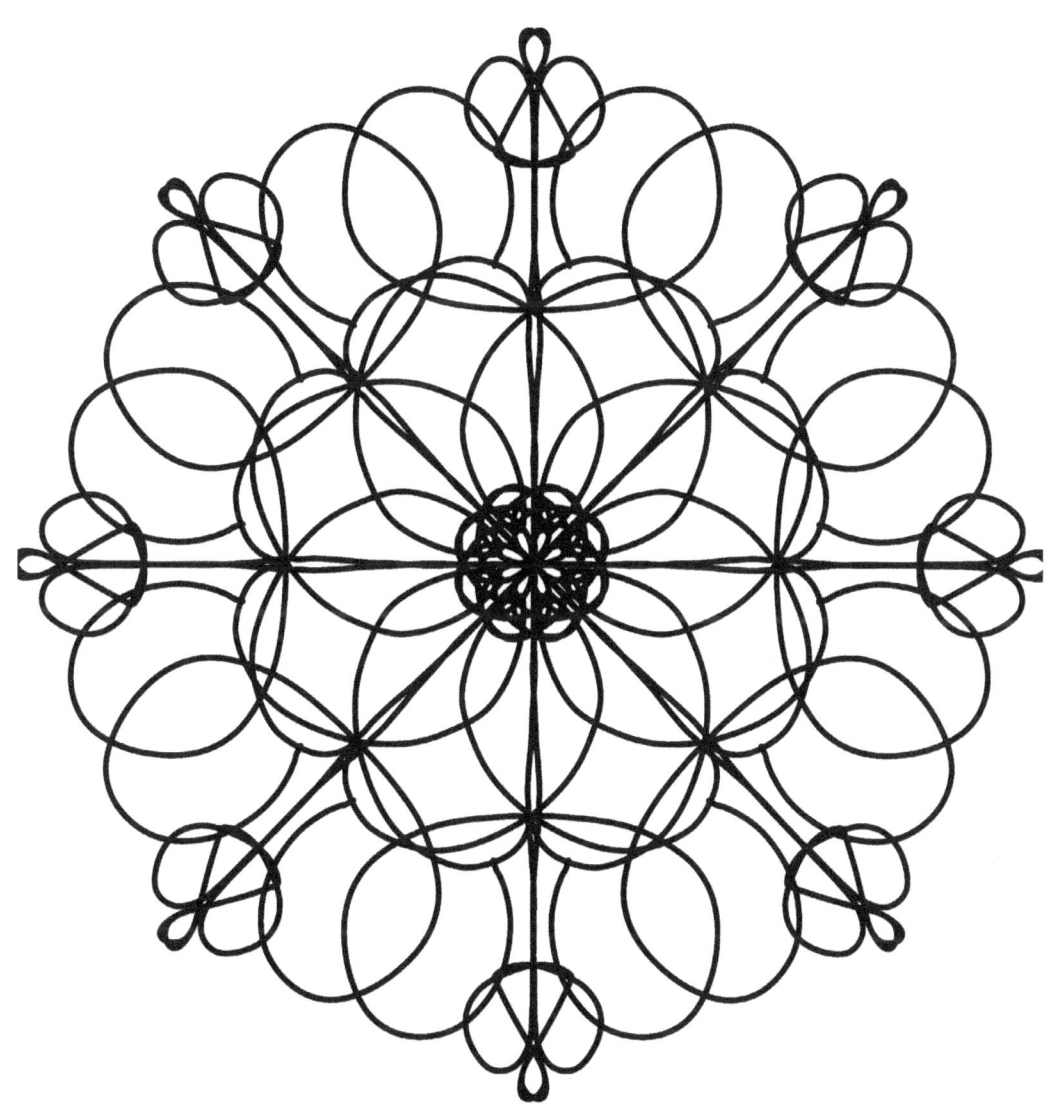

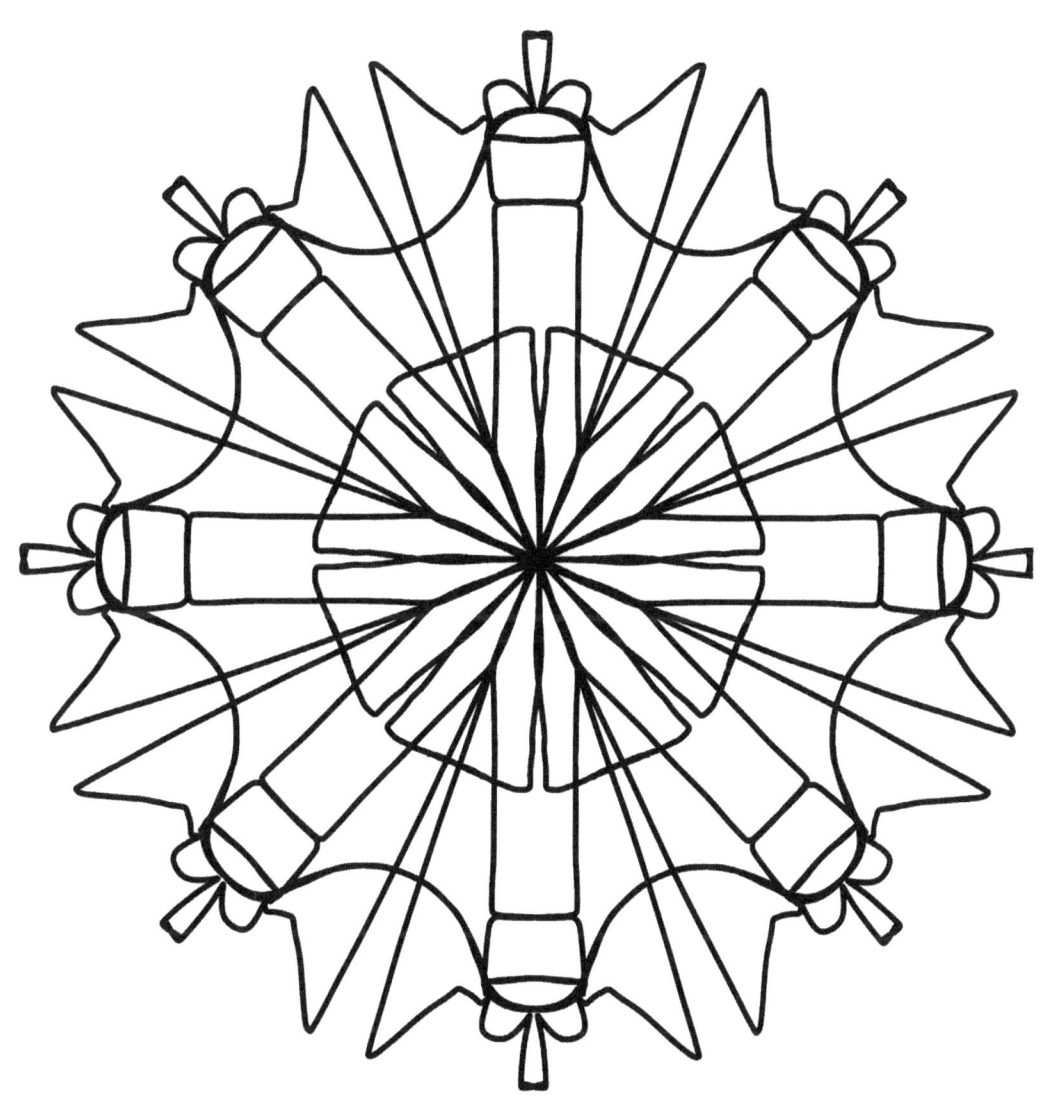

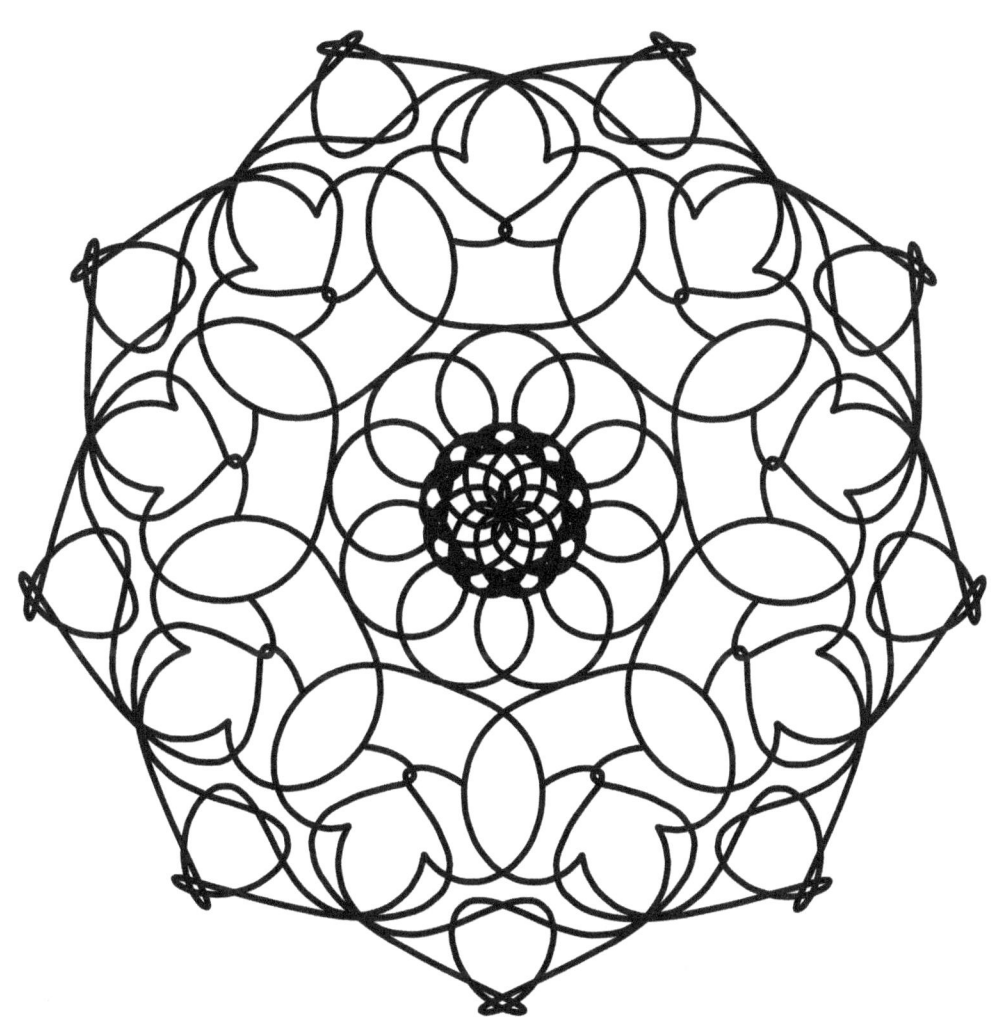

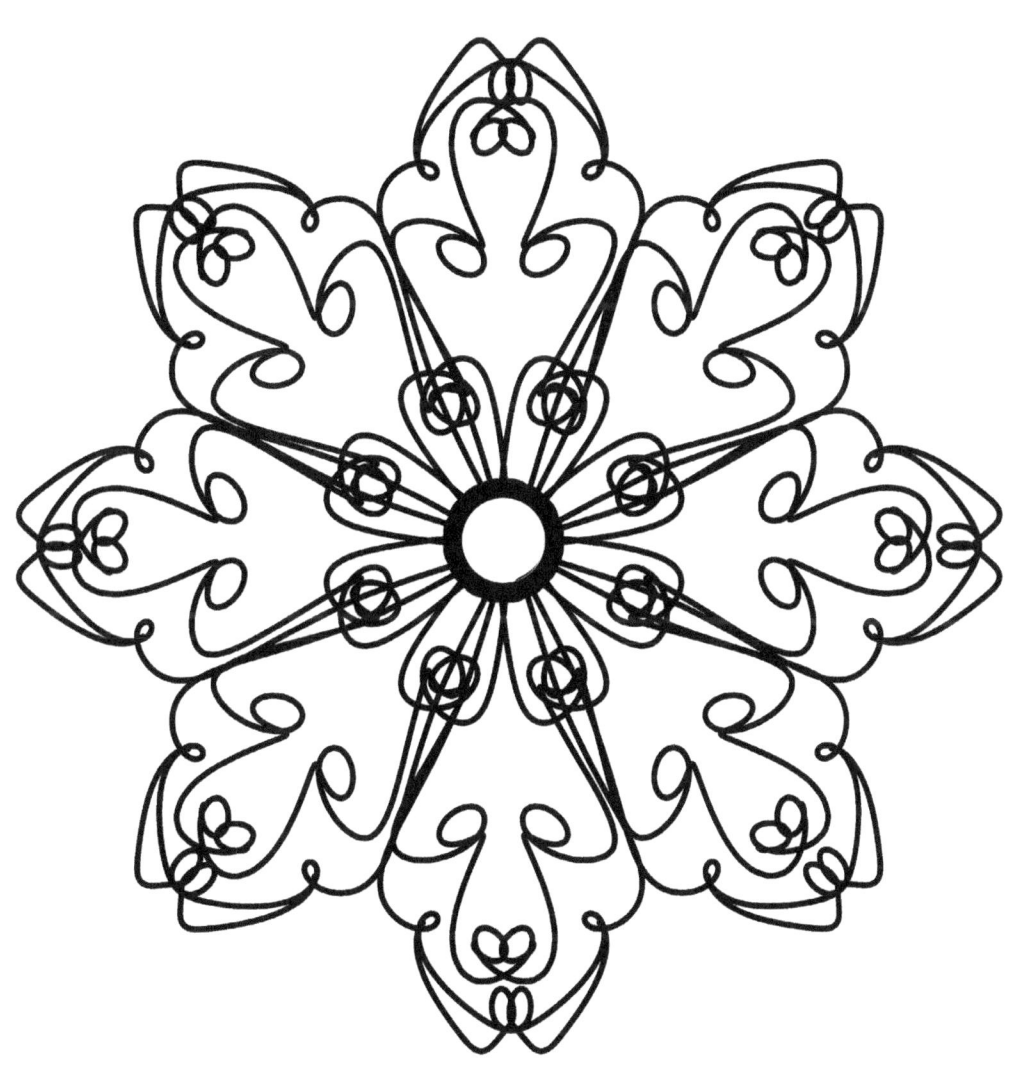

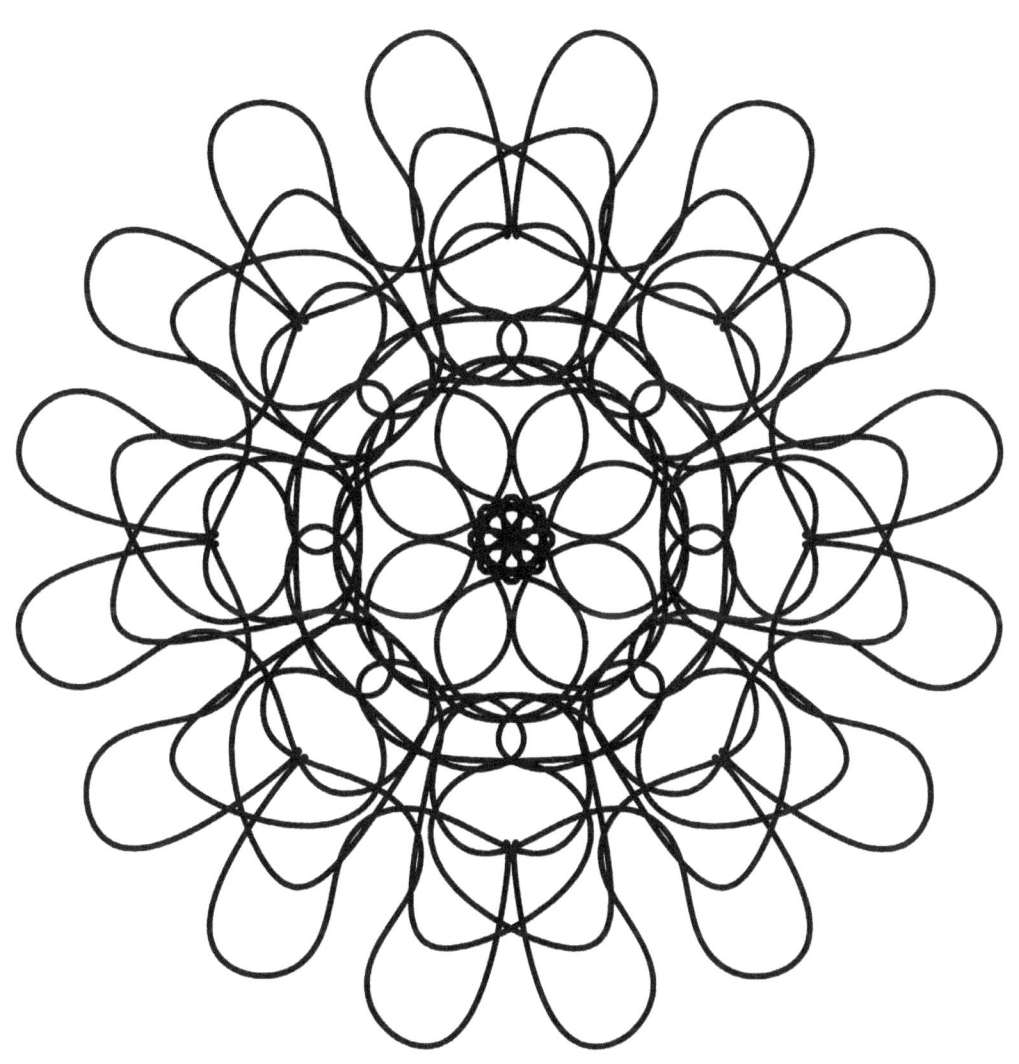

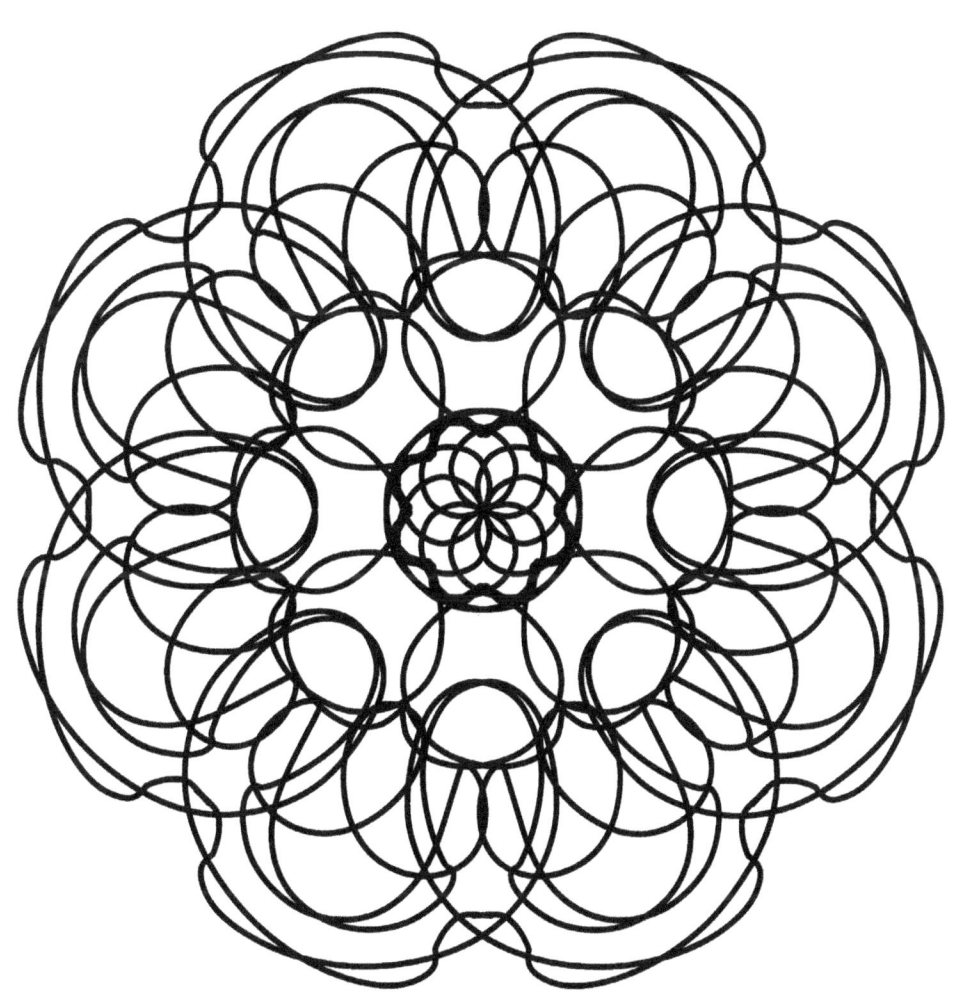

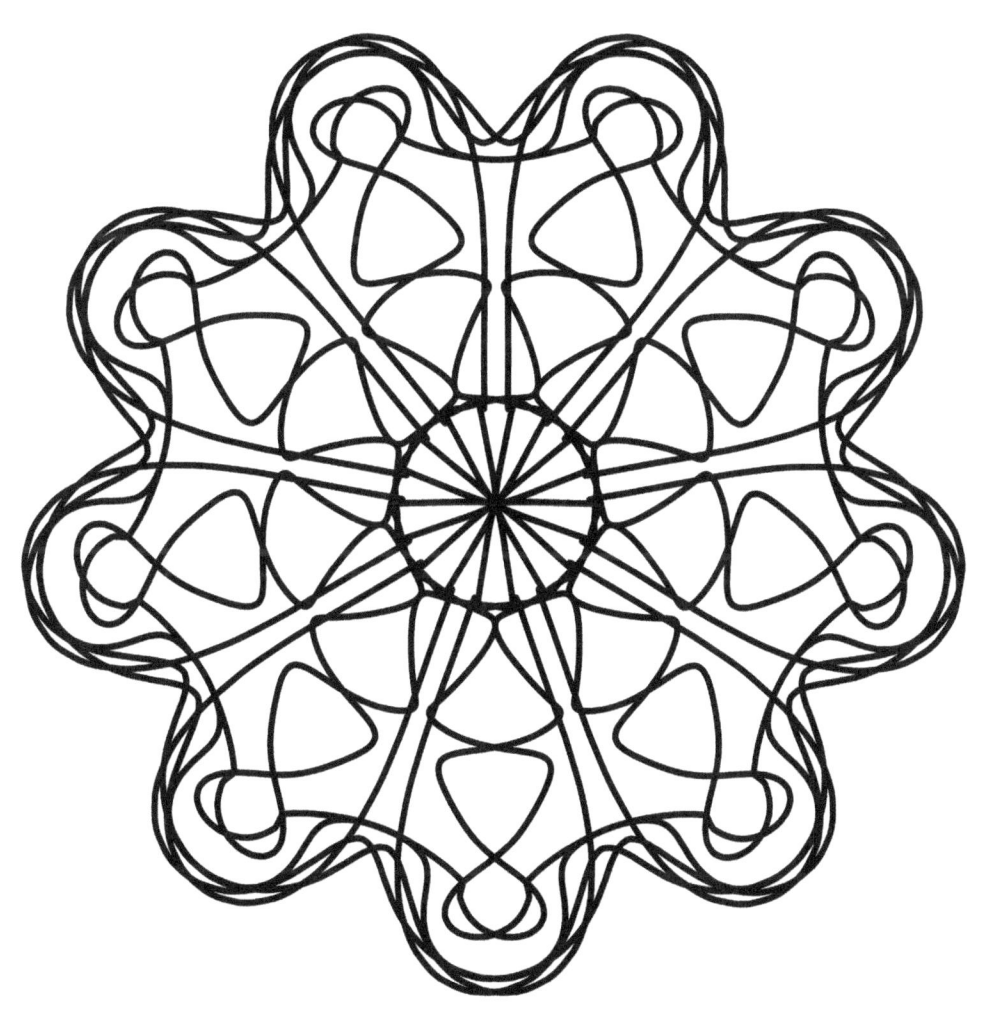

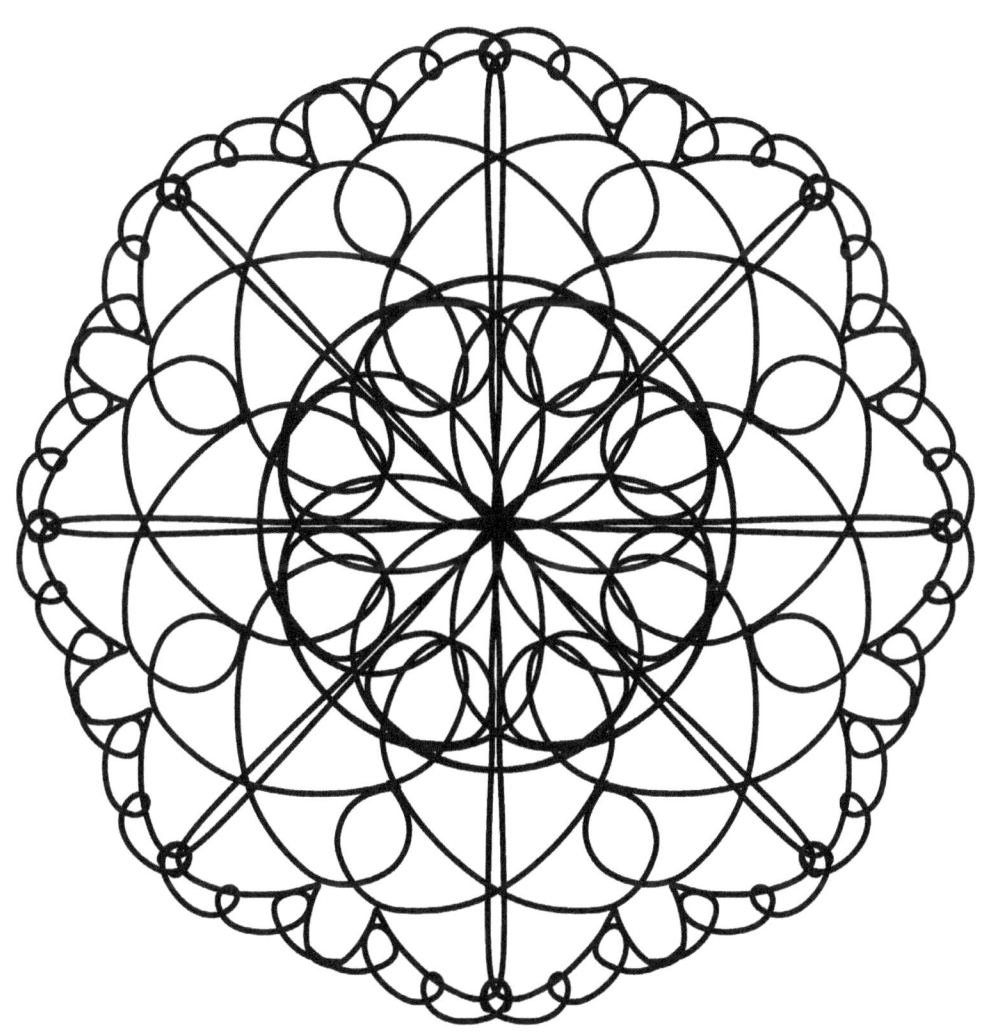

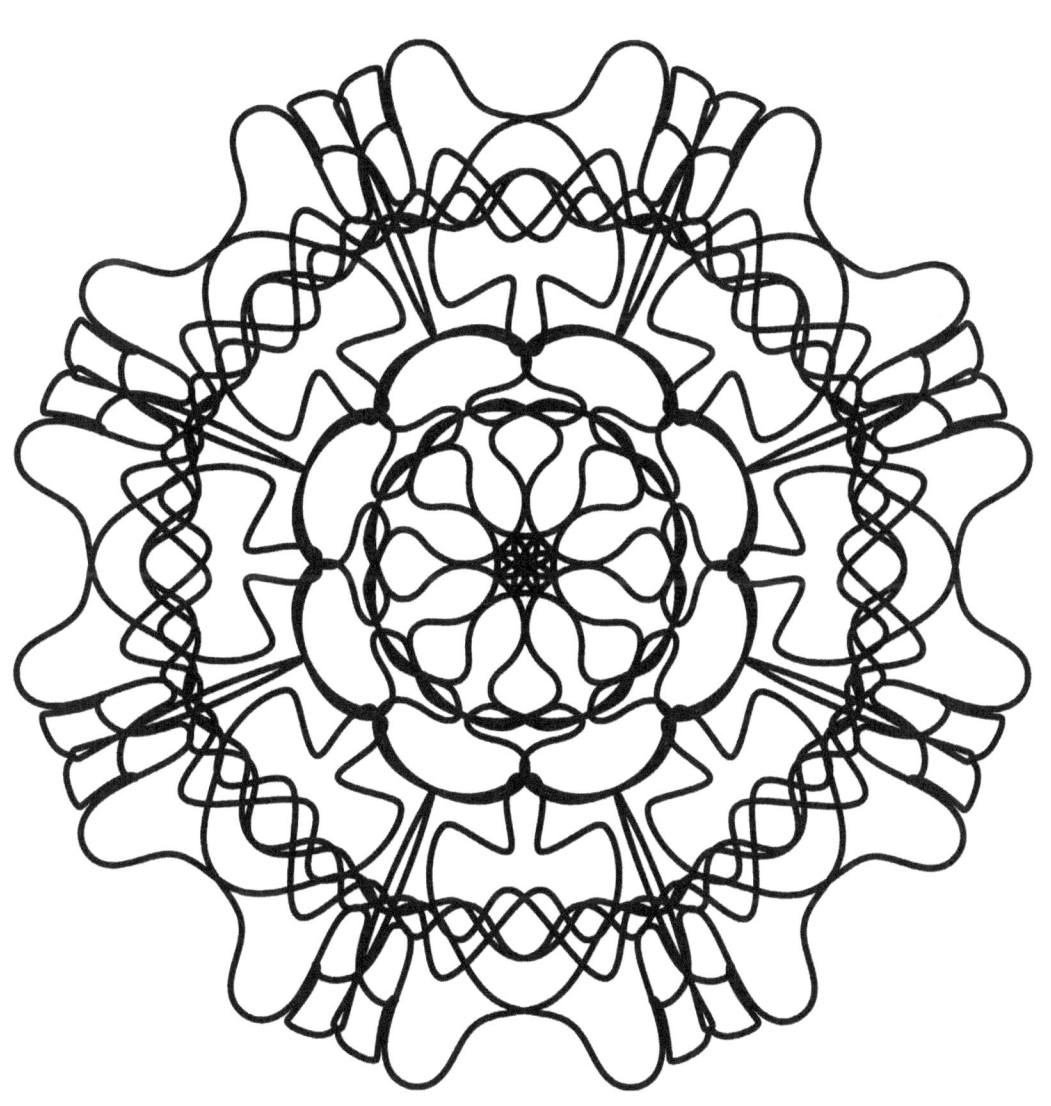

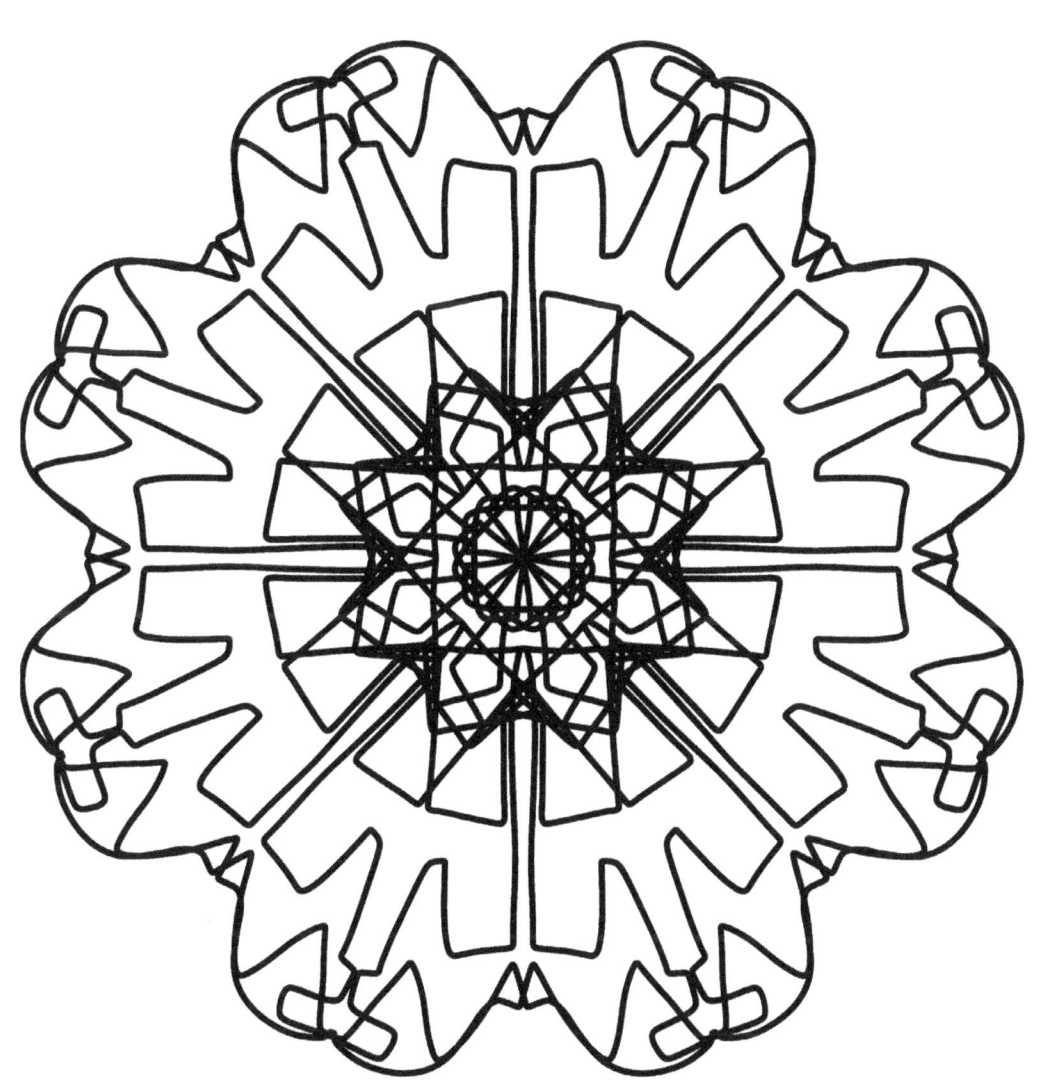

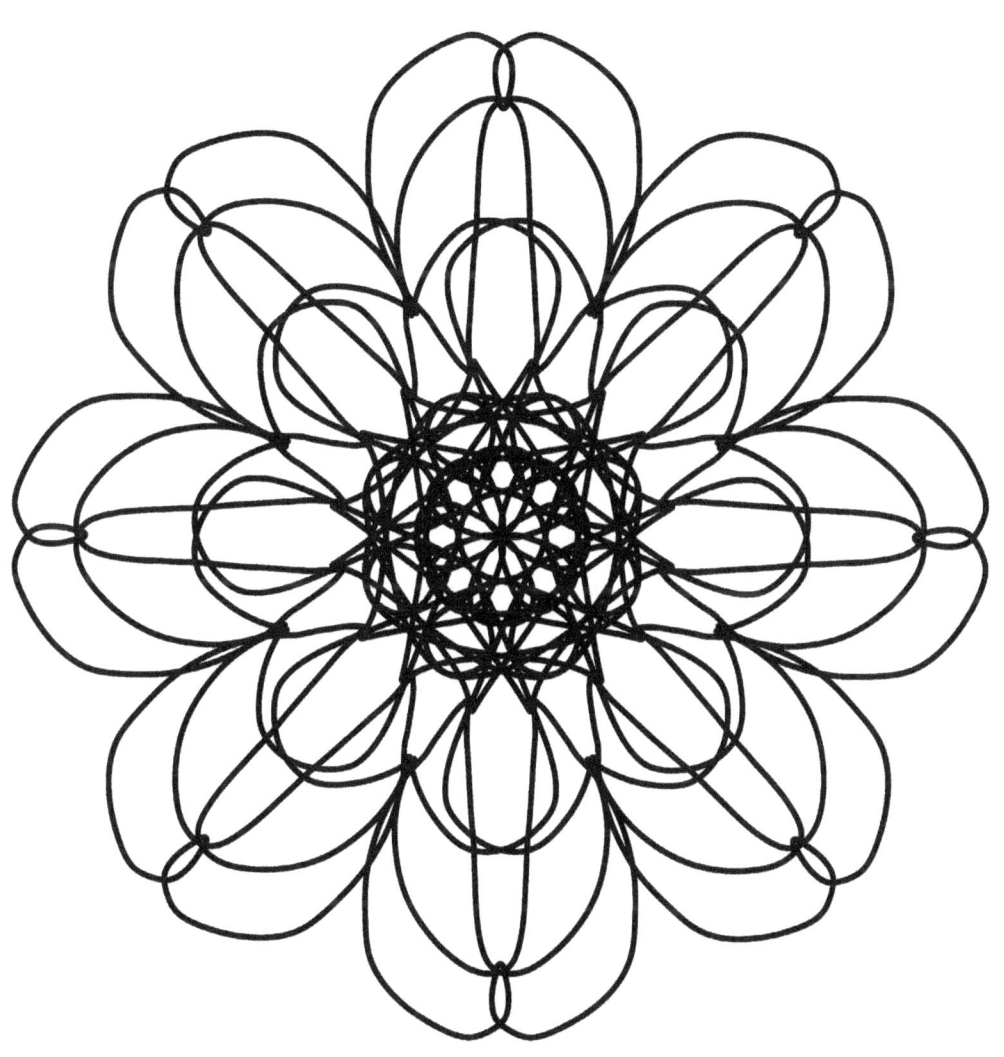

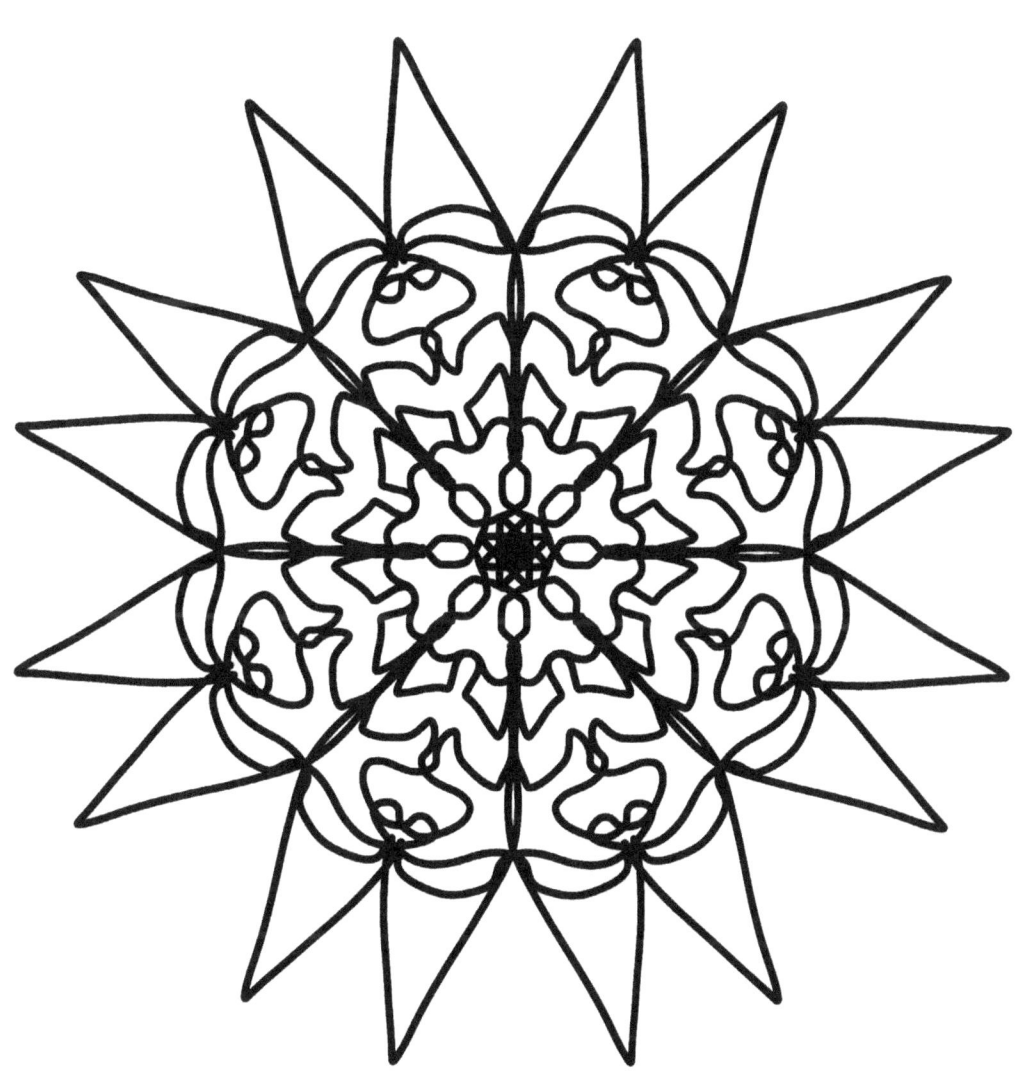

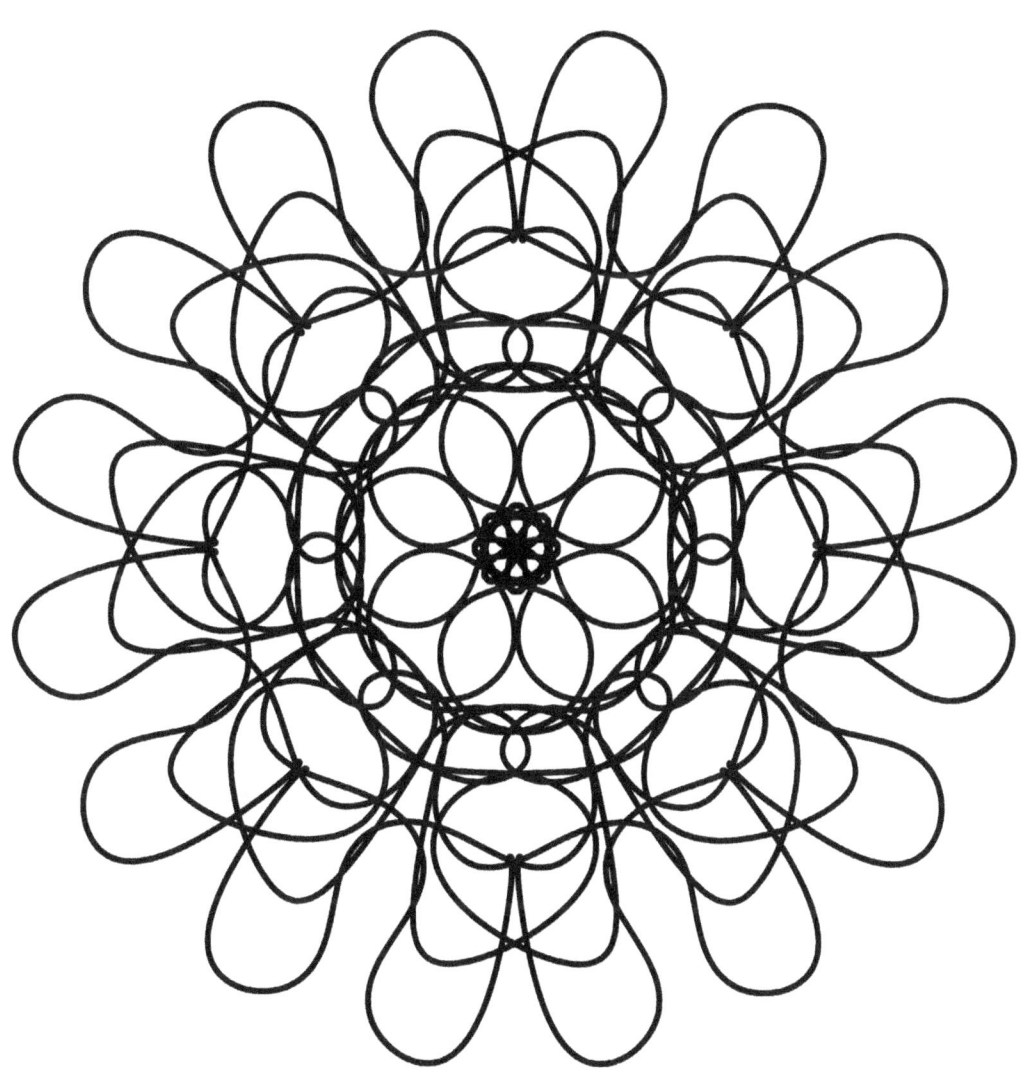

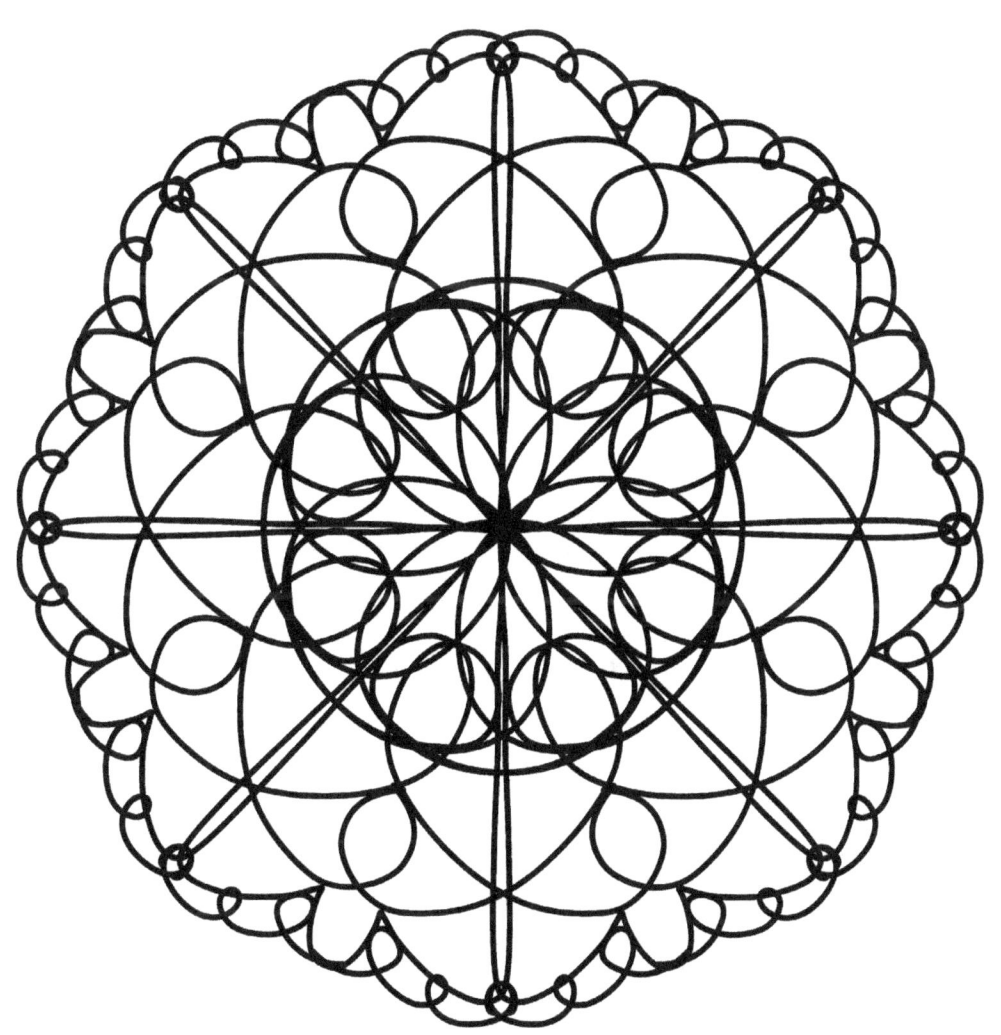

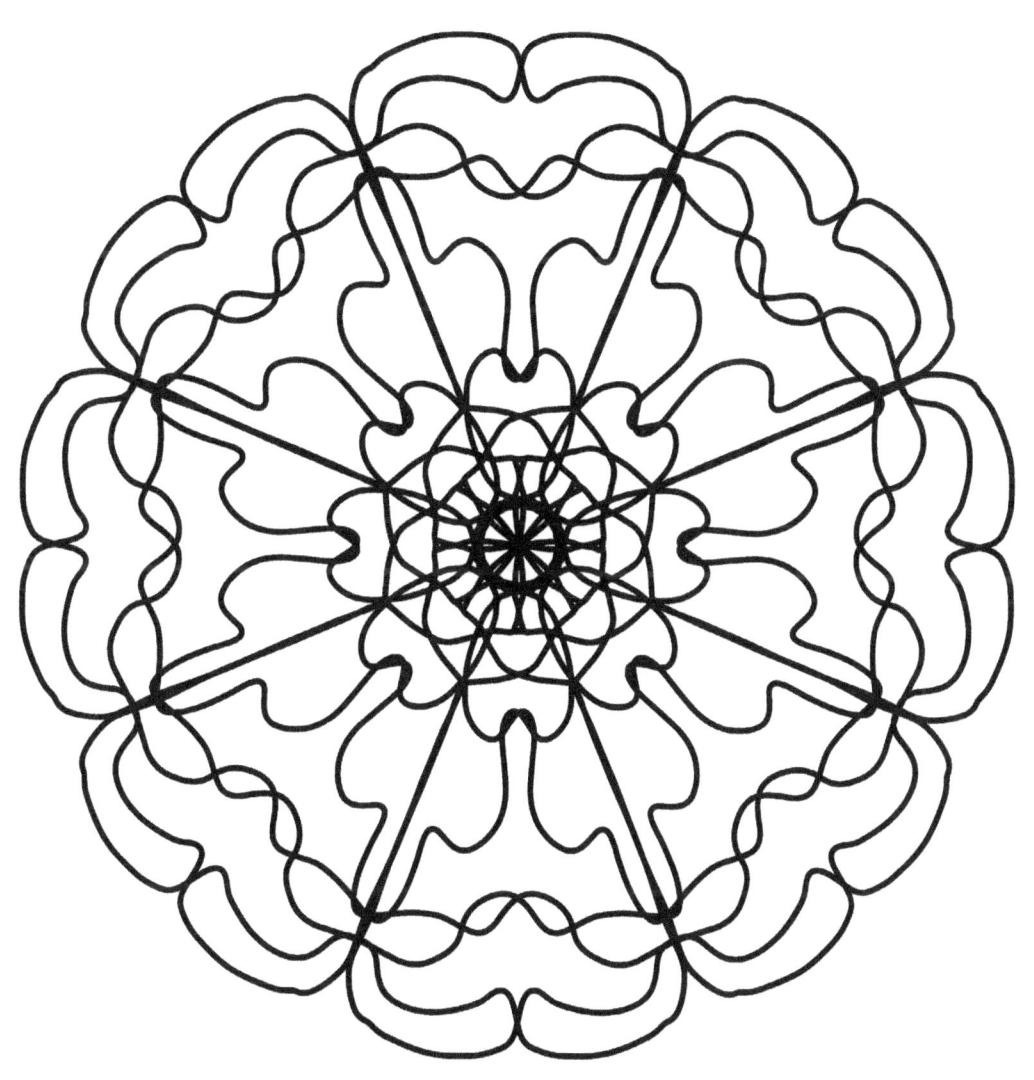

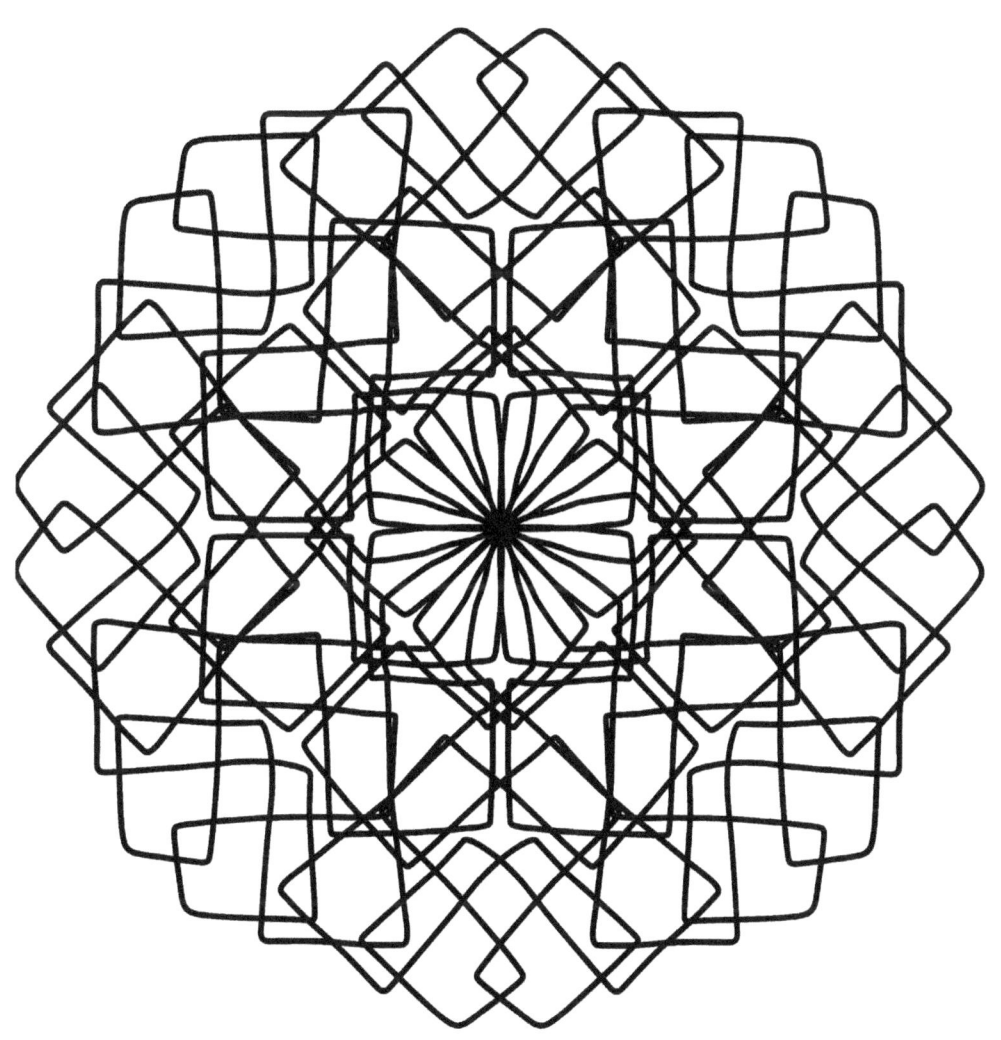

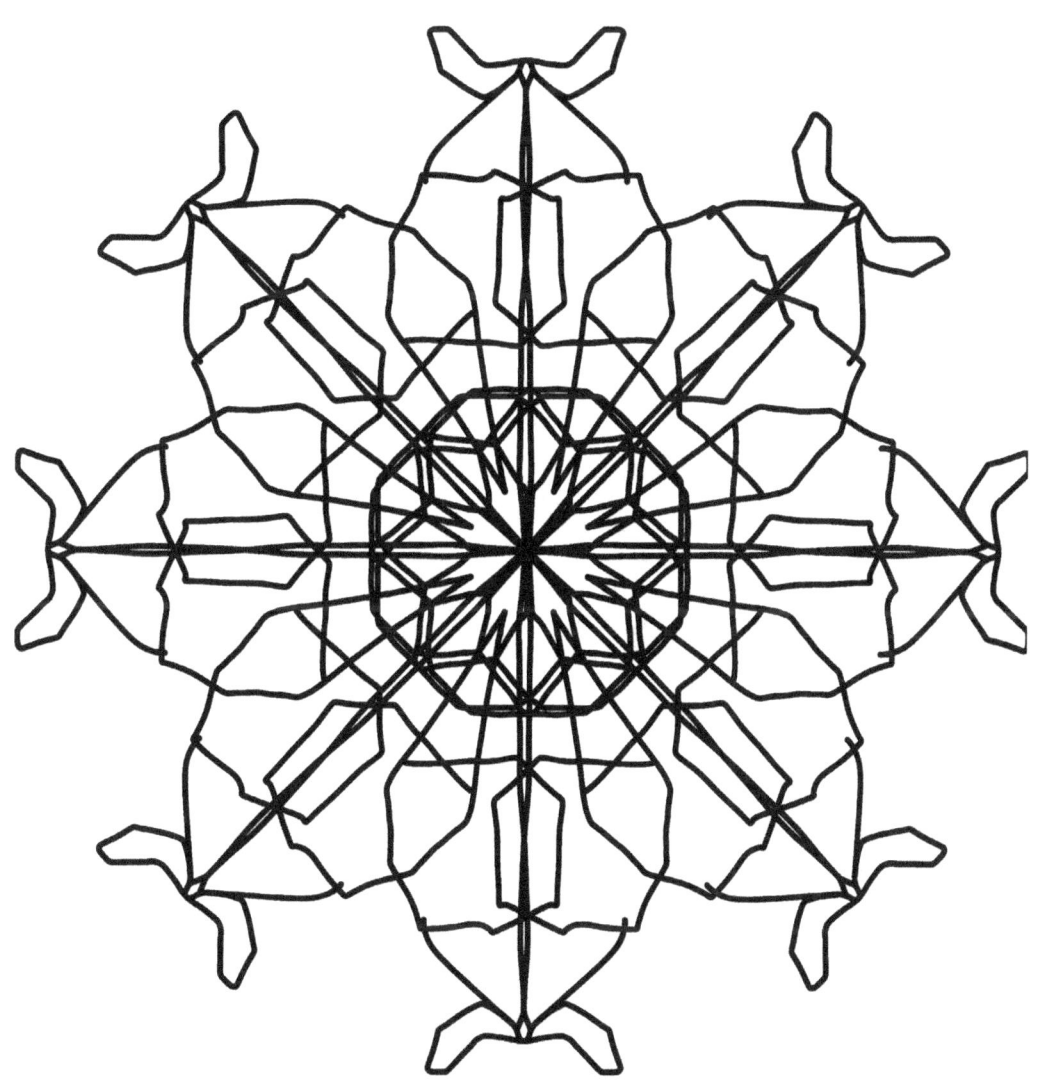

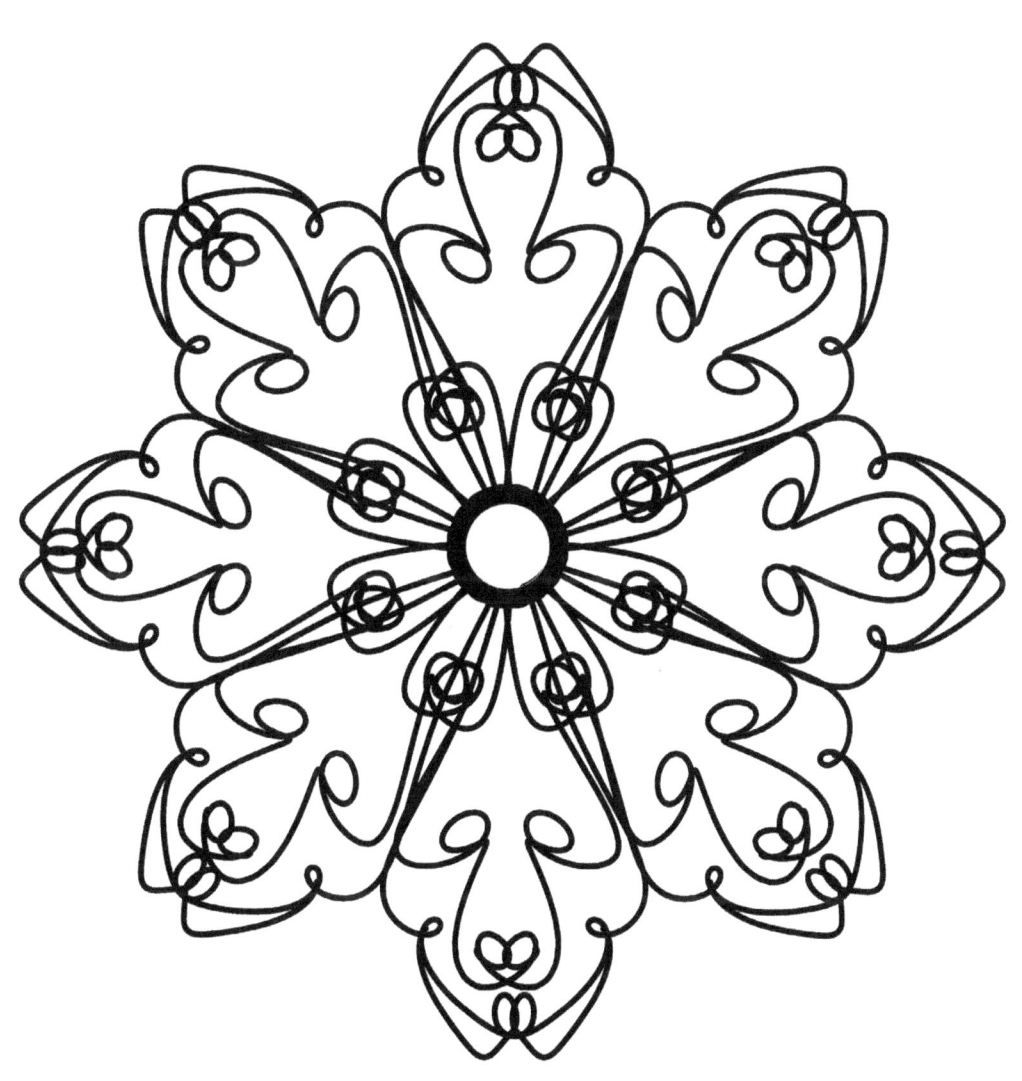

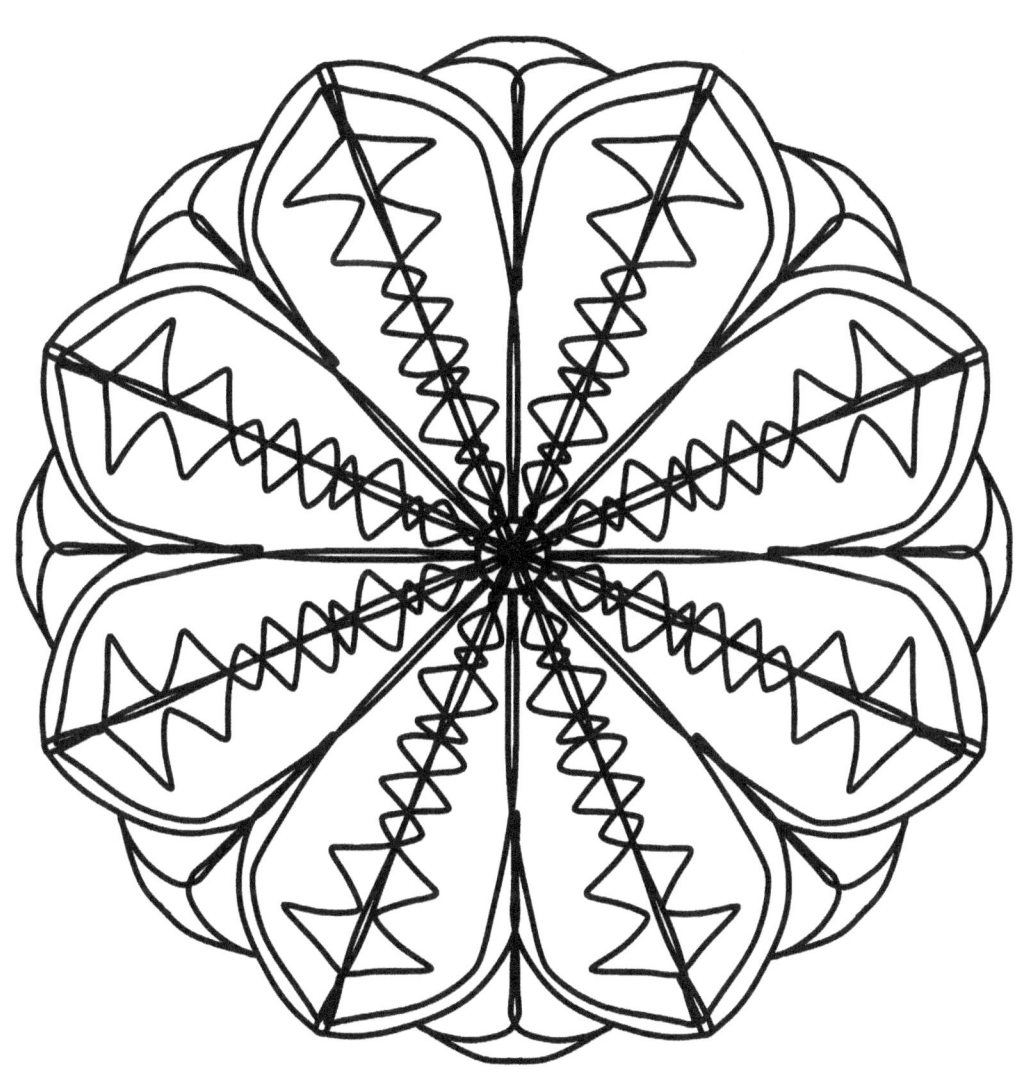

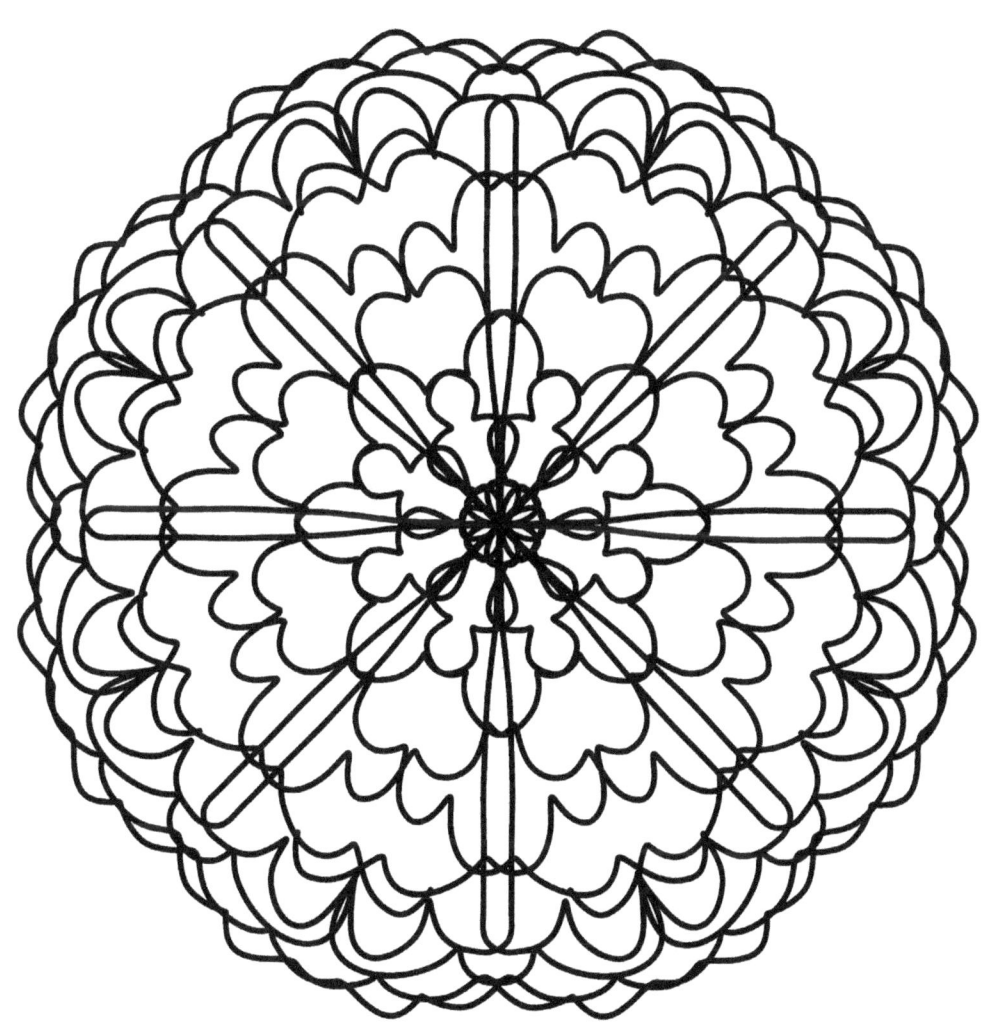

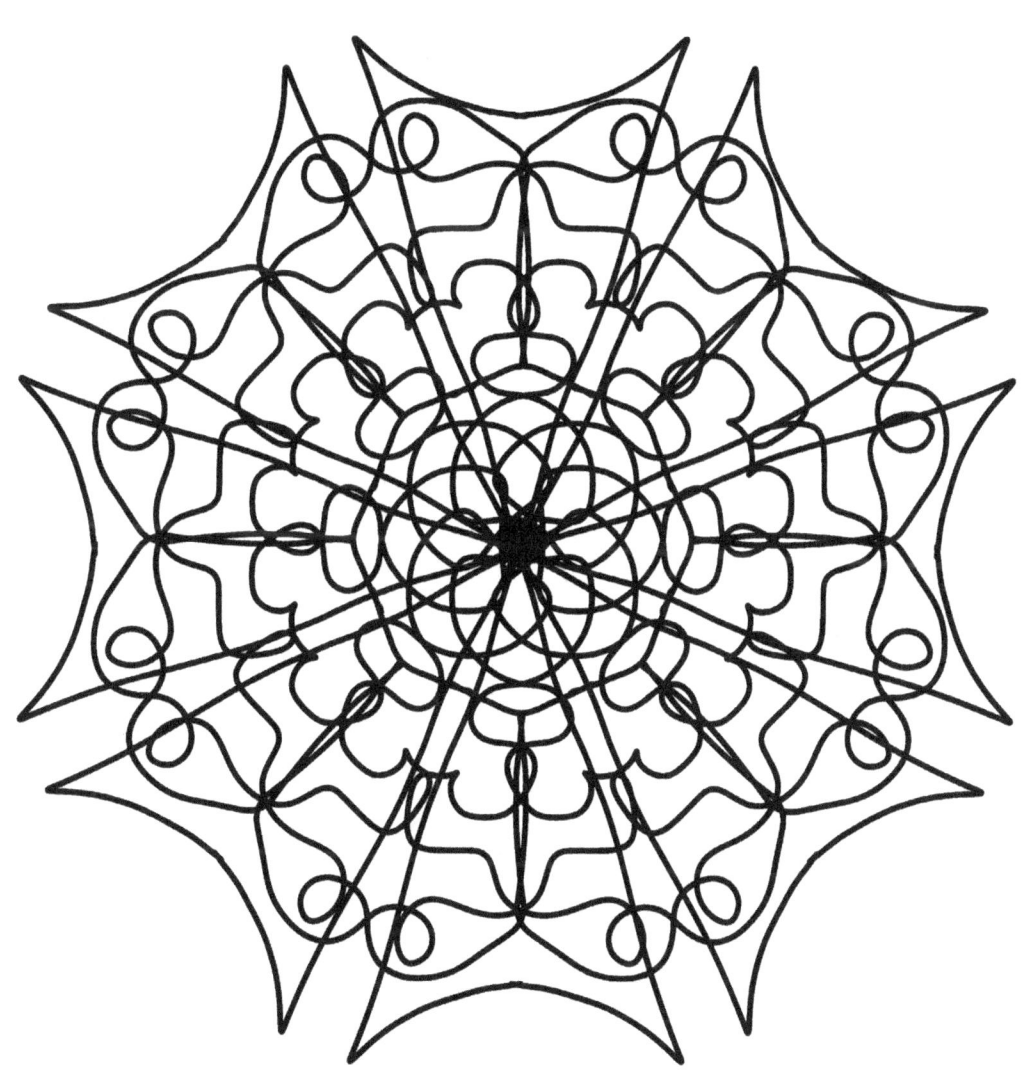

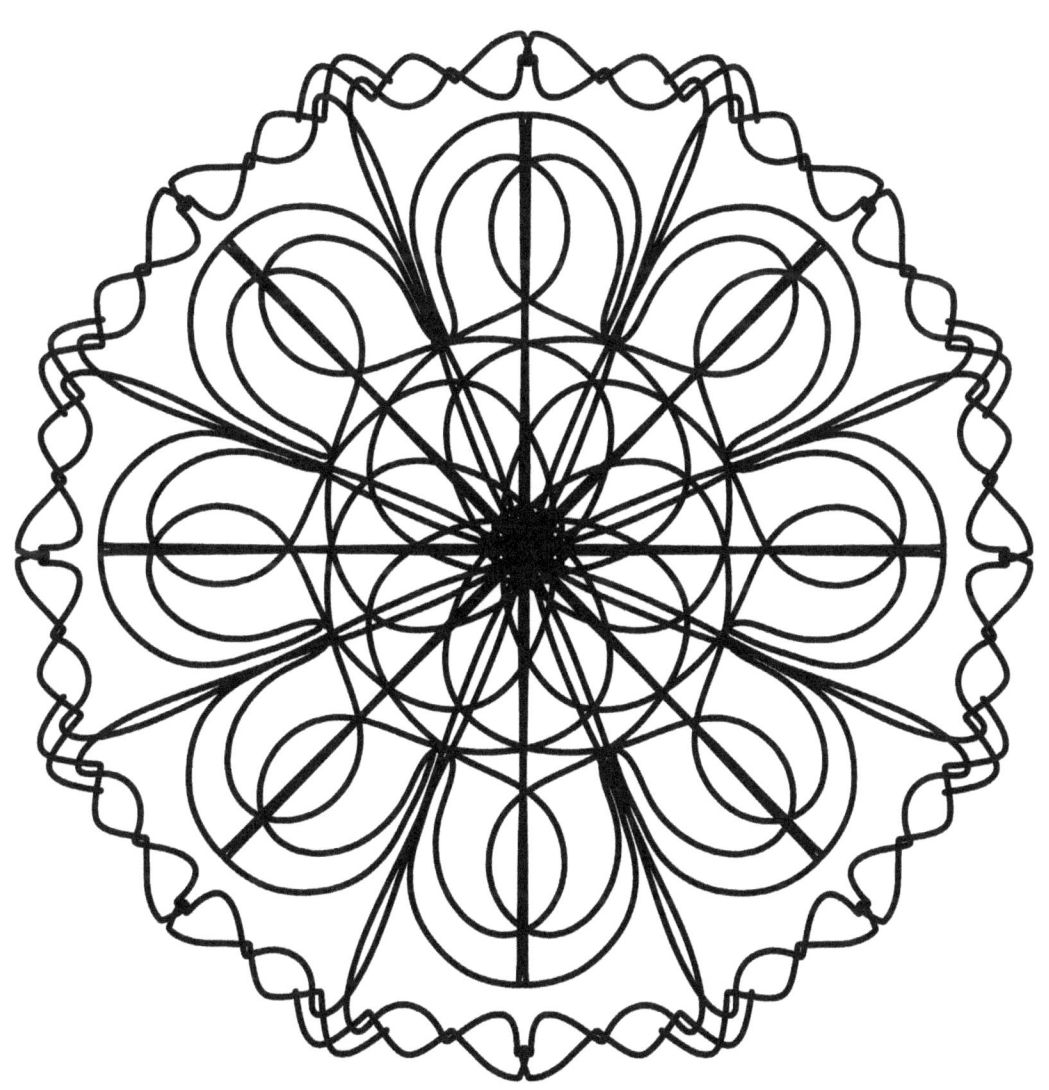

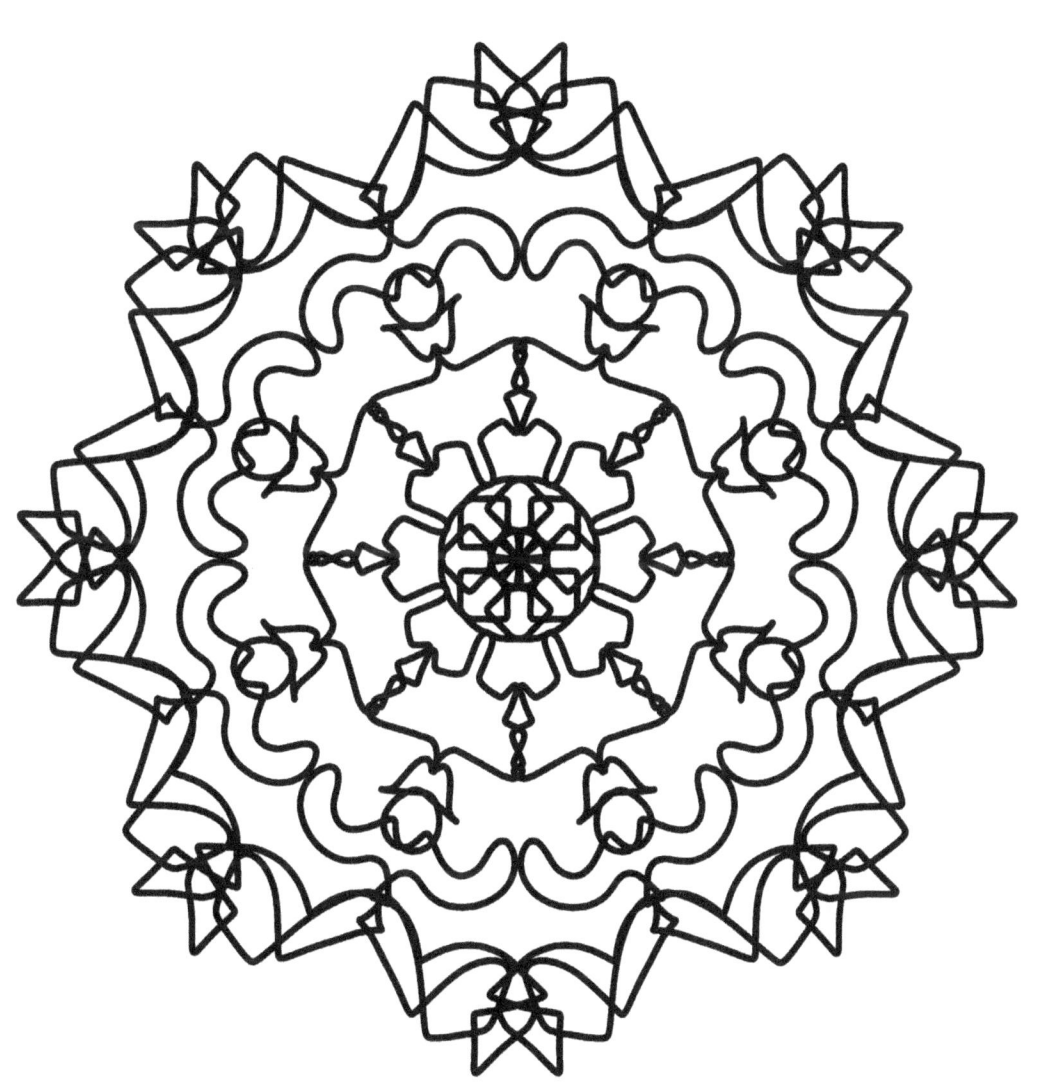

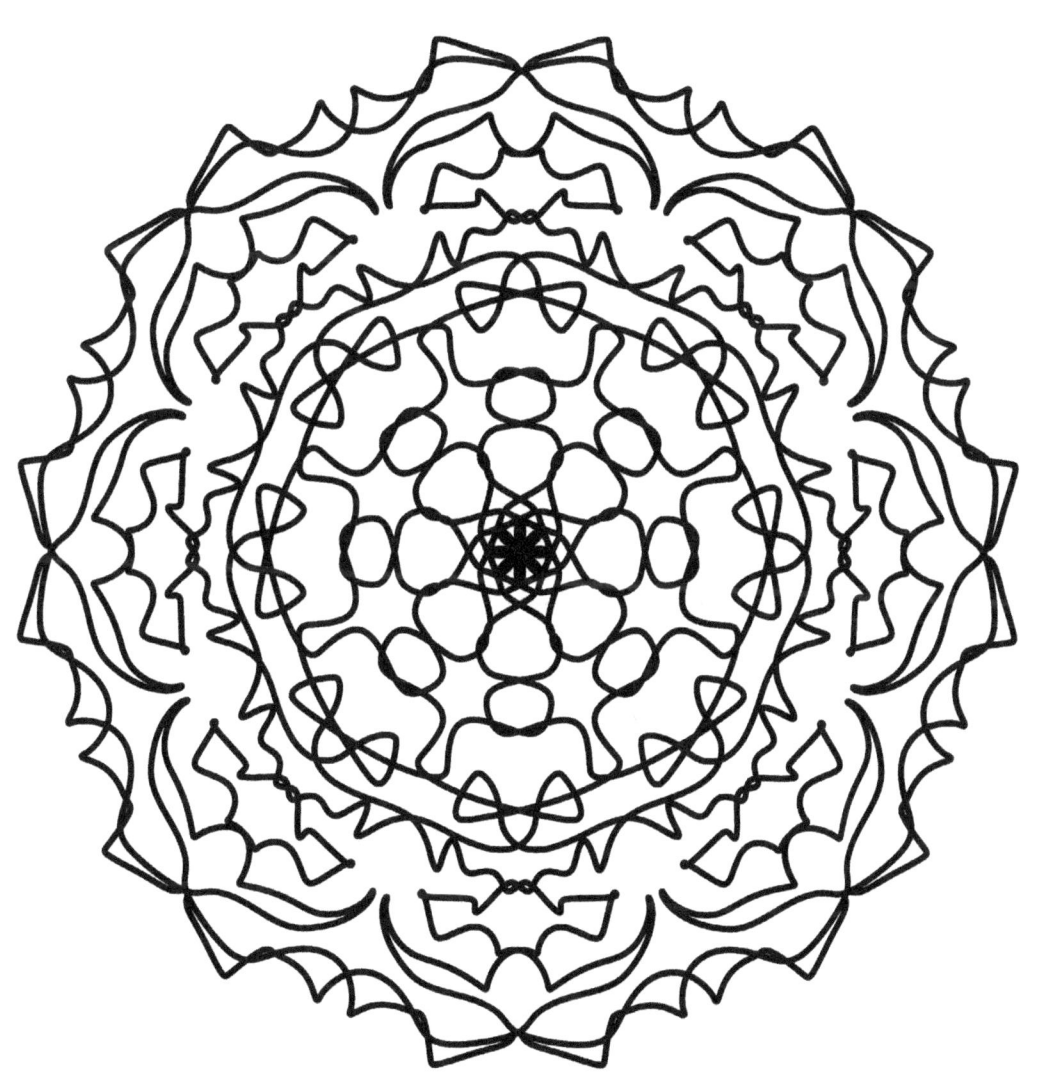

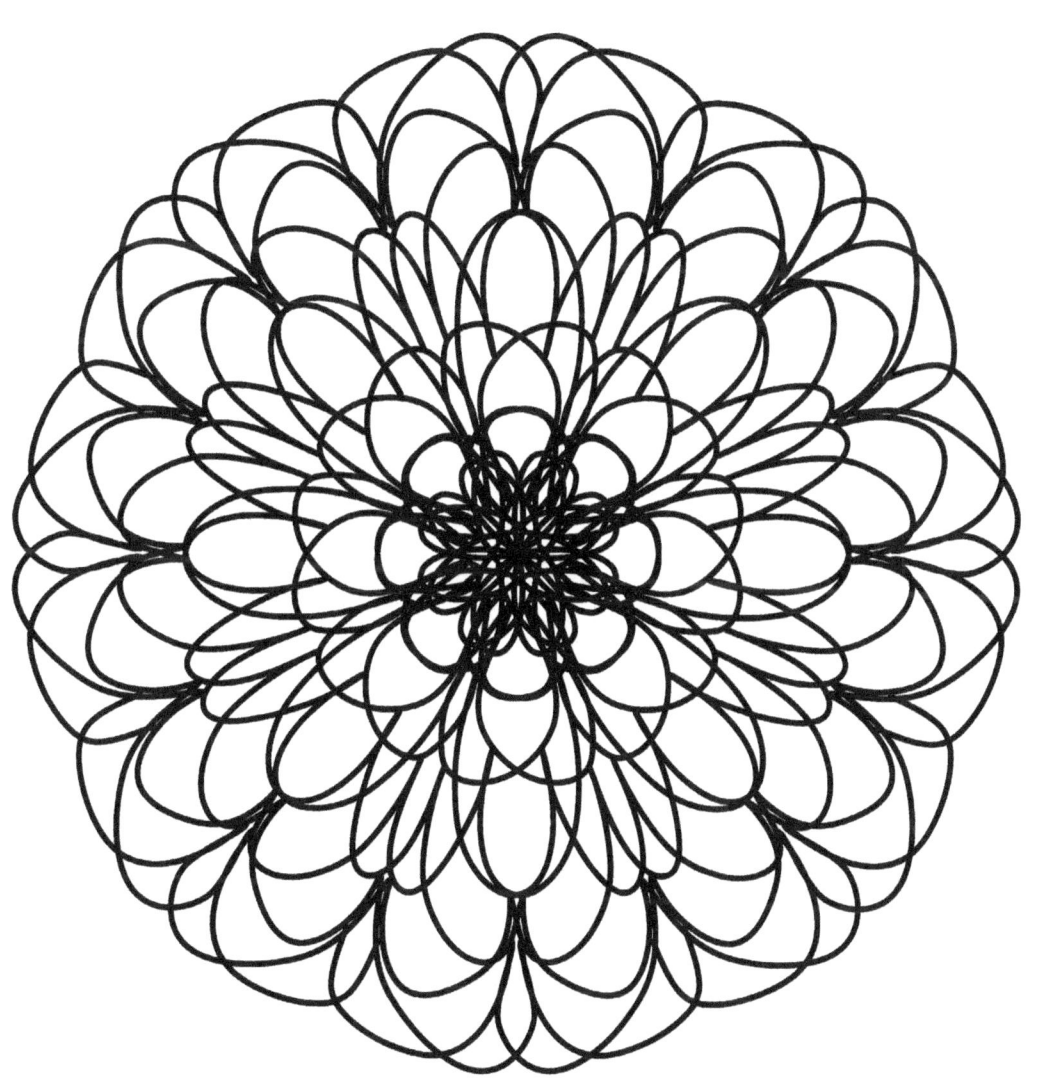

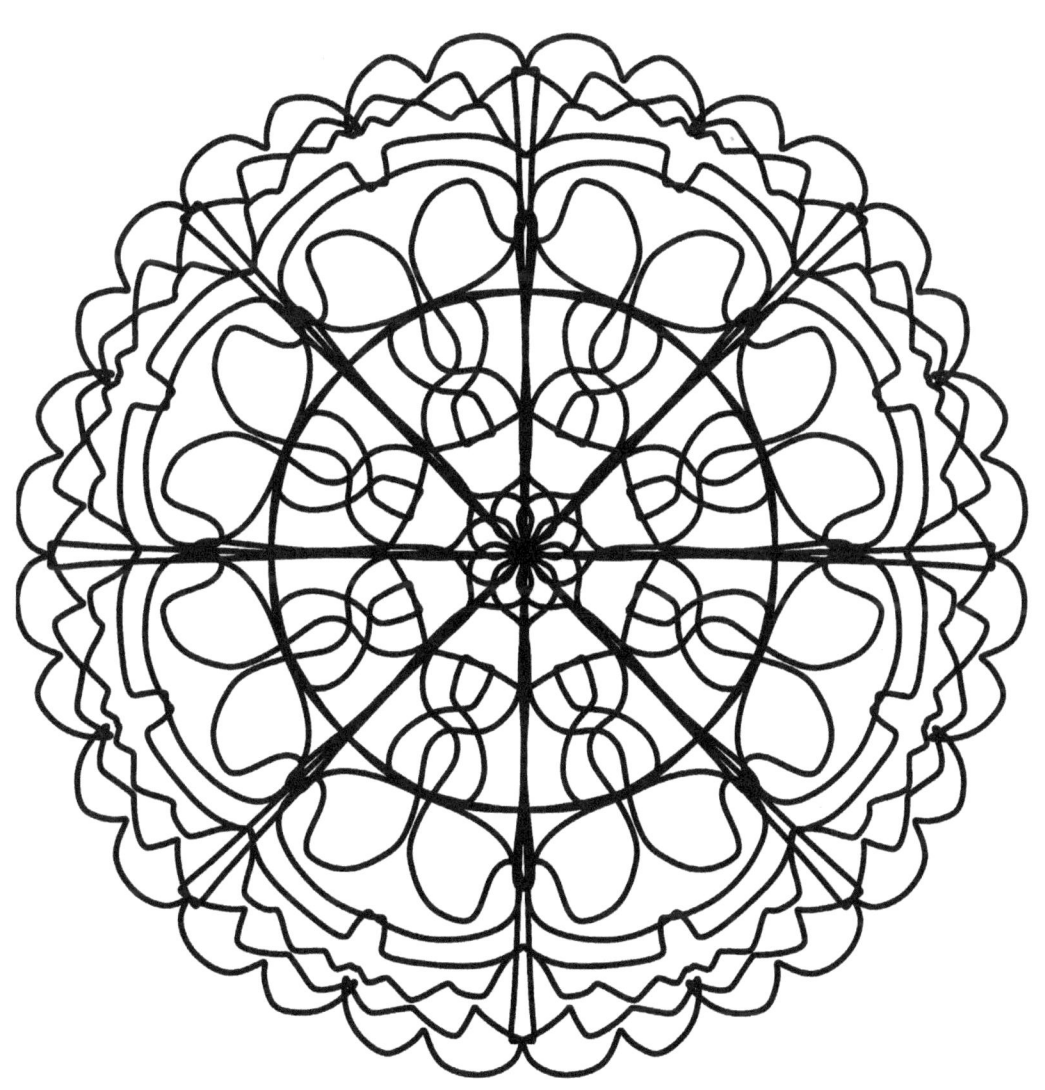

Test Page Here

Use the space below to test colors and your mediums weight before you start.

Test Page Here

Use the space below to test colors and your mediums weight before you start.

Test Page Here

Use the space below to test colors and your mediums weight before you start.

Dedication

This book is dedicated to all people that think they are not creative. I believe with all of my heart, that each and every individual is uniquely creative in some way. All it takes is dedication and a little practise to see amazing results of your chosen medium, be it in the arts, entertainment, using words or inventions from the mind, it is all up to you to choose.

www.ingramcontent.com/pod-product-compliance
Lightning Source LLC
Chambersburg PA
CBHW081845170526
45167CB00007B/2904